THE

THINKING

DILEMMA

A MANIFESTO ON LIVING A LIFE OF HAPPINESS, SATISFACTION, AND PURPOSE

The Thinking Dilemma

Copyright 2016 by Kyle Willkom

Printed in the United States of America
ISBN-13: 978-1523302925
ISBN-10: 1523302925

This book is dedicated to young people everywhere.

You have the opportunity to build the life you imagine.
I hope this book helps you do so.

Foreword

I've known Kyle since our Freshman year of high school. We became good friends and challenged each other often to improve in all areas of our lives.

Kyle has continued to challenge high school students to improve, and he will challenge you to think from the moment you start this book.

In my career I have found that the single most important talent I can control is my mind. This involves deep thought and self control of my mental state. Being in control of my mental state has given me the ability to be present, to be in the moment, which is vital on and off the soccer field.

Kyle talks in this book about the distractions of life; it may be a feud with a friend in the past or the fear of going to college. I've found that taking time to think and be present will free you from past drama and eliminate those future pressures.

Kyle not only helps you understand the importance of thinking but also gives you the guidance to ensure your thinking is positive and meaningful.

When you start to think, you start to live.

Ethan Finlay

Ethan Finlay
MLS All-Star

Wake Up Call
5 Essential Lessons They Won't Teach You in School

A novel about Dillon, a student whose life gets turned upside down by an unexpected twist of fate. His next steps lead him on a fantastical journey that teaches him life-changing lessons he could not have learned any other way.

Learn more at:
ActionPackedLeadership.com

Acknowledgments

Thank you to my family: Monte, Patti, John, Bryan, Erin, Anna, Josh, Vincent, Fiona, Walter, and counting. I love you all, and wouldn't be where I am without your support.

Thank you to Tim Fandek, Terri Mackey, Keegan O'Brien, and the rest of Wisconsin DECA for consulting me often and making a positive difference in young lives.

Thank you to the people who helped review this book, specifically Breanna Speth, Hannah Trudeau, Kyle Stanley, Daniel Klingelhoets, and David Fornetti. Your thoughts and feedback are always appreciated.

Thank you to those who have helped with my writing through the years, specifically Madeline Guyette, Kayla Spencer, Ruby Thompson, and Lorenzo Munoz.

Thank you to Mike Lee for pushing me to always pursue my dreams, Tanner Olson for your entrepreneurial spirit and for helping me stay grounded, and Tracy Anello for your thoughts and insights in every area of my life.

Thank you to Ethan Finlay for the foreword and for always being there for me.

Thank you to all of my friends and extended family who have supported me through the years, your uplifting words and encouragement mean a great deal to me.

And last, but not least, thank you God, for everything you have done in my life.

Preface

This book will not tell you everything.

If you are looking for heavy stats and in-depth research, you will not enjoy this book. This book is a start – a call to action.

The format of this book is not typical. Major points are emphasized heavily and minor points have been excluded for the sake of brevity. In this way, you may be longing for more depth.

This is where you come in.

The depth of this book comes from you – your personal reflection and application of the topics presented. You are in charge of changing your life.

I want you to read this book. I want you to have thoughts and conversations about the topics within it. But more than anything, I want you to know that you have the ability to intentionally choose your path to happiness, satisfaction, and purpose.

I hope your journey does not end when you finish this book. I hope that you continue to apply these concepts every day, and work to make your world brighter.

I hope this book provides the spark you need to overcome the thinking dilemma and build the life you have imagined – a life of happiness, satisfaction, and purpose.

THE
THINKING
DILEMMA

A MANIFESTO ON LIVING A LIFE OF HAPPINESS, SATISFACTION, AND PURPOSE

Meet Dan.

Dan is a junior in high school and is pretty normal. He has a girlfriend, Amy, and a small group of friends. Dan plays the trumpet in the school band, which is about the only time of day he is motivated to be in school.

Life is not always the easiest for Dan, as it is not very easy for any high school student.

For example, there are some people in his high school that Dan absolutely hates. One of them is Tyler, the captain of the football team. In Dan's mind, Tyler could get expelled tomorrow and shipped off to military school and the high school would be a much better place.

Close behind Dan's hatred for Tyler is Dan's hatred for Tyler's girlfriend, who is coincidentally also named Amy. This girl could fall off a cliff for all Dan cared. She is a smart girl and is the Vice President of the National Honor Society, but something about her seems snotty and stuck-up to Dan, and he hates her.

Worse yet, is when Tyler and Amy are together. The pictures they post of themselves online make Dan want to throw up. If he has to see one more picture of Amy kissing Tyler after a football game, he's going to lose it.

Dan is ready for high school to end. He wants to get out. Knowing that he has an entire year left before graduating seems like an eternity, and he can't stomach the idea of going through the same boring classes with the same annoying classmates any longer.

But what Dan has failed to realize is that he can change his scenario anytime he wants.

This is where the thinking dilemma begins.

The world has a huge problem.

No one thinks anymore. We are too distracted by the world around us to stop, reflect, analyze, and change our surroundings.

We have phones, tablets, video games, social media, TV shows, movies, and a thousand other things that keep us distracted enough throughout the day to keep us moving forward, but never allow us time to think about what matters.

If we don't solve this problem, we're in big trouble.

This is:

The Thinking Dilemma

High school students aren't good at thinking.

There, I said it.

No one is good at thinking. People are good at a lot of things, but thinking is not one of them.

People don't sit in silence and think, especially high school students. It doesn't happen.

When was the last time you sat alone just to think?

Students are good at watching Netflix, talking about social media, and pretending to pay attention to the people who are actually around them.

But thinking? Not so much.

The thinking dilemma has hit us hard.

High school boys daydream about girls, and high school girls return the favor. Students watch videos and laugh at them or open Snapchats and respond to them.

But there isn't a whole lot of **real**, in-depth thought going on.

In a study that I'm making up right now, students do lead the world in several capacities. These include:

Zoning out.

You may have already zoned out once or twice since starting this book.

Being incredibly social and antisocial at the same time.

I'm sure you know people who post on social media more than they talk to the people around them.

Adding unneeded drama to the world around them.

Really though.

Among others.

Dan has become overwhelmed with the people around him and the life he is currently living. Tyler and Amy are just one example. He doesn't know how to change his life, mostly because he hasn't put any thought into how he could change it.

Just about every day, Dan spends a good amount of time gaming. He zones out playing Call of Duty or FIFA and before he knows it, hours have passed. He games with friends, but it's not like there are lively discussions taking place when they play.

Dan spends time scrolling through his Twitter and Facebook feeds every day and looks through Snapchat stories whenever he's bored.

Interestingly enough, Dan hasn't said a word to Tyler or Amy in person in about three months. His hatred for them is actually pretty ridiculous. He sees their constant updates on social media and gets upset with each new post. He then gets reminded daily of the annoying couple and their life together when his friends bring them up in band.

Dan has fallen into a trap, along with everyone else in the world. He can only get out of this trap when he realizes he is in one.

He is living his life thoughtlessly. He is a victim of the thinking dilemma.

But don't take my word for it.

Think about your friends. Really, close your eyes and do it.
But open them back up to read the questions below.

How many have shown you something meaningless on social media in the last two days?

How many of them complain about their parents or teachers in the course of a given week?

How many consistently repeat things they saw in videos, shows, or movies?

These are primary indicators of thoughtlessness. They all consist of information and content that was fully thought out by someone else or rely on an outlook of negativity.

These mindless thoughts are at the core of our issue.

Now ask yourself a different but similar question:

How many of your friends have started a conversation with a statement like:

I had an interesting thought yesterday...

or

I've been thinking lately about...

and then followed this statement up with something of substance?

Students are drawn to drama and entertainment, but never take the time to think, analyze, or reflect.

They say whatever it is they see or hear, and there is a **very clear** problem with this:

No one wants to be **John Madden.**

Let me explain.

John Madden was a football announcer known for being incredibly basic. That is exactly what you have become if you add nothing of value to a conversation.

Here are six real John Madden quotes, just to give you an idea of how basic he was.

1. "When you have great players, playing great, well that's great football!"

2. "Here's a guy, here's a guy who when he puts his contacts in, he can see better."

3. "If this team doesn't put points on the board I don't see how they can win."

4. "If you lose your best cornerback and punter, I'd say that's a double loss."

5. "The Dallas Cowboys have 2 types of plays in their playbook. Passing plays, and running plays."

6. "Whenever you talk about a Mike Shanahan offense, you're always going to be talking about his offense."

Dan is surrounded by John Madden comments every single day, although they don't revolve around football. His friends say things like, "This new show got 5 stars; it must be pretty good." Yeah. Obviously. Dan doesn't think anything of this lack of thought because these comments have become the norm.

While he might not want to admit it, Dan is bored.

The times he feels happiest are when he is with Amy (his girlfriend; not Tyler's Amy) - when they have dinner together or break up their routine by taking a spontaneous adventure. In these moments, he experiences a joy that takes him out of the unhappy monotony of the rest of his high school experience.

But Dan hasn't reflected on why he's so happy in those moments and so unhappy elsewhere. He continues to go about his life in the same way he always has. Video games. Social media. Boredom. He just casually thinks that's the way his life is and that he has no power to change it.

Dan is completely wrong.

He can change his life at any moment, but he first needs to believe there is value in making a change. More than anything, at this moment, he needs to understand why he should think.

We absolutely need to start thinking. But before I tell you how we should think, we need to answer the question:

WHY?

Why should we care about thinking?

Technically, that's two questions, but it's the same thought. You get the idea.

Anyone can talk about an idea someone else had or something on social media someone else created.

We've grown accustomed to "Retweeting" thoughts.

What about your ideas?

What have you created?

This takes thought.

But as I've said...

Students aren't good at thinking.

Although, it may not be their fault. They've never been given a real reason to truly think.

So let's answer the question:

Why should we think?

If you had to answer this question, what would you say?

Think about it.

Have friends of yours ever said things like,

"Maybe I'm just overthinking it?"

Or have you ever wondered about something, whipped out Google and had the answer in ten seconds?

If **overthinking** causes problems, and Google makes **under thinking** so easy, why should you think at all?

The answer to this question lies in one word:

HAPPINESS

It continues with the word "Satisfaction," but we'll get to that later.

Our **thoughts** direct our **actions**; our actions direct our **lives**.

> Anyone who has ever achieved a seemingly unreachable goal knows that it all starts with a dream (the most optimistic form of thought); a vision of what could happen that affects what actually happens.

Our thoughts can be:

positive or negative

complex or simple

real or imagined

And the beauty of this is that we get to decide.

No matter what type of thoughts we have, they will **always** affect our happiness and our lives by driving our actions.

Dan's thoughts are negative, and these thoughts don't truly depict the world around him. He is choosing to think this way, and this choice is making him unhappy.

Dan is completely responsible for how he views the world around him, and he hasn't done a good job of choosing positive thoughts.

An example of this is the last time Dan talked to Tyler. Dan was standing at his locker as Tyler and his friends were walking by. Tyler was laughing about something and jokingly gave a little push to one of his buddies. His buddy gave him a push back sending Tyler directly into Dan. He didn't hit Dan too hard, but hard enough for Dan to drop a notebook on the ground.

Tyler quickly picked up the notebook, "Sorry about that, Dan."

"Come on, Tyler."

"Hey man, I didn't mean to hit you like that."

"It's alright."

Tyler handed Dan his notebook then walked away and continued laughing and joking with his friends.

Dan could have chosen to brush this moment off and believe that Tyler truly didn't mean it, but instead he let this interaction fuel his negativity toward both Tyler and Amy. He chose a negative thought.

Dan still hasn't had his moment of clarity – the moment when he realizes how important thinking is to creating a happy life.

David Foster Wallace can tell you all about how thinking can impact your happiness and how negativity can be overcome if we choose to think more intentionally. Below is an excerpt from his commencement speech at Kenyon College.

I've cut to the middle to get to the point.

"If I choose to think this way (negatively) in a store and on the freeway, fine. Lots of us do. Except thinking this way tends to be so easy and automatic that it doesn't have to be a choice. It is my natural default setting. It's the automatic way that I experience the boring, frustrating, crowded parts of adult life when I'm operating on the automatic, unconscious belief that I am the center of the world, and that my immediate needs and feelings are what should determine the world's priorities.

The thing is that, of course, there are totally different ways to think about these kinds of situations.

In this traffic, all these vehicles stopped and idling in my way, it's not impossible…that the Hummer that just cut me off is maybe being driven by a father whose little child is hurt or sick in the seat next to him, and he's trying to get this kid to the hospital, and he's in a bigger, more legitimate hurry than I am: it is actually I who am in HIS way.

Or I can choose to force myself to consider the likelihood that everyone else in the supermarket's checkout line is just as bored and frustrated as I am, and that some of these people probably have harder, more tedious and painful lives than I do.

Again, please don't think that I'm giving you moral advice, or that I'm saying you are supposed to think this way, or that anyone expects you to just automatically do it. Because it's hard. It takes will and effort, and if you are like me, some days you won't be able to do it, or you just flat out won't want to.

But most days, if you're aware enough to give yourself a choice, you can choose to look differently at this fat, dead-eyed, over made-up lady who just screamed at her kid in the checkout line. Maybe she's not usually like this. Maybe she's been up three straight nights holding the hand of a husband who is dying of bone cancer. Or maybe this very lady is the low wage clerk at the motor vehicle department, who just yesterday helped your spouse resolve a horrific, infuriating, red-tape problem through some small act of bureaucratic kindness.

Of course, none of this is likely, but it's also not impossible. It just depends what you want to consider. If you're automatically sure that you know what reality is, and you are operating on your default setting, then you, like me, probably won't consider possibilities that aren't annoying and miserable. But if you really learn how to pay attention, then you will know there are other options... you get to decide how you're gonna try to see it. This, I submit, is the freedom of a real education, of learning how to be well-adjusted. You get to consciously decide what has meaning and what doesn't. You get to decide what to worship."

Dan's band instructor, Mr. Olsen, notices the drama that has been unfolding throughout the year. He decides to keep Dan after class and have a short conversation about it.

"Dan, why do you and your friends talk so much about Tyler and Amy?"

"I don't know..."

"Do they say things to your group? Do they make jokes about you being in band?"

"No. They're just annoying."

"So other than them living the way they want to live they haven't done anything to you to make you hate them?"

"I don't know."

"Dan, your grade in band is suffering."

Now Dan starts paying attention.

"You have been giving more attention to things you have no control over than the things that actually matter. You could be a great trumpet player, but you're wasting time moping around and being negative. I'm sorry to say it like that, but I think you know it's true. This drama is not productive for you."

The conversation with Mr. Olsen isn't earth-shattering for Dan, but it does make sense. For the first time, Dan starts to realize that he can choose his thoughts, and that they don't have to be so negative or dramatic. He has a brief moment of clarity that opens the door to living a happier life.

In order to choose what you think, you need to first admit that it matters. This is at the core of the thinking dilemma.

Your thoughts matter.

They determine how you see the world.

They have the ability to direct your happiness.

If you don't choose to think,
your natural default setting will become one of negativity, frustration, and unhappiness.

When you choose to think, you become more in control of your own happiness through simple awareness.

This positive awareness naturally translates to positive actions and interactions.

Dan wants to be happy, or happier than he currently is at least. The conversation with Mr. Olsen wasn't easy to hear. The fact that his grades are suffering makes him uncomfortable, and what's even more uncomfortable for Dan is that he knows Mr. Olsen is right.

Dan's negative thoughts are affecting everything. He now understands why he should think.

He decides to take steps in the right direction. He starts by asking his girlfriend if she'll help him stop being so negative.

She pretends to not know what he's talking about as she stares at her phone, "What do you mean?"

"I'm making myself unhappy. I'm only thinking about things that upset me. It's like I'm choosing to be negative."

Having never thought about the thinking dilemma before, Amy doesn't know how she's going to help Dan think differently. She doesn't fully understand why it matters, but Dan now knows that it matters a lot.

Dan tries to convince Amy to care, "Have you ever noticed how much we talk about Tyler and Amy? We don't even hang out with them. Why does their relationship have to determine my happiness? I want to be happier than that."

Amy isn't fully convinced about anything because she was only half-listening in the first place, but she wants to help Dan because he's her boyfriend and he asked her for help.

"Okay, Dan. Where do we start?"

Thinking changes our lives by directing our actions.

Because we know this is true, there is a second natural question that needs to be answered:

What should we think?

Picture yourself at this very moment, exactly as you are.

Now picture a perfect version of yourself.

What would change for you to be a better version of you?

This is an exercise based in thought. To properly answer the question above, you must first answer these questions:

How is the best way to be?

How is the best way to live?

Take a moment to answer these questions.

People always say things like:

I'd get better grades.

I'd be more popular.

I'd lose weight.

I'd have more money.

I'd be dating someone special with a beautiful face, body, personality, and pretty much perfect in every way.

It's okay to dream.

Self-evaluation is a vital step in directing your thoughts.

Seriously, what are your answers to these questions?

How **do** *you* want to be?

How **do** *you* want to live?

Push yourself to think about your goals and less about how society views success and happiness.

You will be most happy, effective, and engaged in your life when you are taking strides toward being the person you envision yourself to be.

Thinking about the best way to be and to live makes a huge difference.

Thought leads to action.

Action leads to outcome.

You cannot be the best version of yourself if you haven't thought about what that version looks like. When you think, you improve.

There are a lot of ways to direct your thoughts.

Once you've figured out the topics that you need to think about in order to be and live your best:

Surround yourself with them!

You can:

Read about them
Listen to podcasts
Talk with people about the topics
Practice them
Join an organization

The more you **think** about the right things, the more your **actions** will reflect them.

Feel free to rip this page out and keep the other side somewhere you will see it often.

Dan tells Amy that he wants to start thinking about the things that make him happiest, and less about the things that get him down. He then starts to evaluate what that means.

He had taken a few business classes in high school, and he likes learning about how the business world works. So Dan asks his business teacher if there are any blogs or business people out there that he could follow to learn more. After getting the list, he decides that whenever he is bored, he will look through social media once (he doesn't want to give it up completely), but then switch over to watching videos or reading blogs about business.

He also decides that he's going to spend more time thinking about music. He loves being in band, and he listens to music all the time, but he doesn't actually think about it all too often. Are there careers in it? How can he improve his playing? He decides to search Netflix for documentaries and films that have a music theme, and he adds them to his list to make sure music plays a larger role in his life.

With these new positive thoughts, he also knows that he needs to remove some of the negative ones. He tells his band friends that he's not going to worry about Tyler and Amy anymore; he's not going to let their social media presence bother him. He's going to try harder not to think about their relationship at all.

Dan has made some significant steps forward.

But he's still not completely happy.

Just a quick recap to make sure you're with me.

1. The thinking dilemma has hit us hard, but you can overcome it
2. Your thoughts are extremely important because they direct your happiness
3. Thinking about how you want to be and live will help you build a better life
4. Thoughts lead to actions

So, assuming you are still with me, you are now thinking about the right things, but you're confused because you're still not completely happy.

That's good, because honestly...

I don't want you to be happy.

At least not all the time.

Happiness comes and goes like any other emotion and it is unrealistic to try to be happy all the time.

It is okay to be sad.

It is completely possible to feel other emotions than happiness and still have a great life.

This is where SATISFACTION comes in.

There is a difference between being happy and being satisfied.

Happiness lasts for a short time. It is one emotion. People have a huge array of emotions in the course of a single day.

People have a huge array of emotions in the course of a single movie.

I'd like you to experience happy moments in your life, but happiness every moment of every day would not be good for you.

People are most apt to feel **happy** when they are spending time with friends or family, traveling, or experiencing something new and refreshing.

If you tried to be happy all the time, there would still be something missing.

You would not be satisfied.

Satisfaction lasts longer than happiness because it comes from the fulfillment of a dream, goal, or desire.

Satisfaction takes work.

Work alone rarely makes us happy.

If people were meant to be happy all the time, there would be no space for work in the world This alone would indicate that the way the world works (no pun intended) is completely backwards.

Work is important because it allows us to find satisfaction through meaningful and purposeful pursuits.

In this way, it can be better to **frown** than to **smile**.

Smiling infers happiness. A determined frown can infer the steadfast, disciplined pursuit of something more meaningful; something that will make us feel satisfied in the long run.

We need to actively think about the pursuits that will make us most satisfied in our lives.

Dan's business teacher notices his newfound excitement for learning and asks Dan what he's thinking about doing after high school.

Dan hasn't really thought about it. He's just ready for high school to end.

Dan's teacher tells him she thinks Dan could do well going to college for business, but that it would take a lot of work to be accepted.

Similarly, Mr. Olsen has been telling him since sophomore year that he could get a scholarship to play trumpet in college if he truly puts in the time and effort.

Up until this point, Dan hadn't thought about going to college or getting a scholarship, but now that he knows it is possible, ho has a vision for what his future could look like. He knows it will take work to get there, but he understands that meaningful pursuits always take work.

Working on his business homework or practicing the trumpet is not easy and won't make him happy in the short term, but Dan now knows it will lead to more satisfaction in the long run.

Dan is thinking better to build a happier life, and is working harder to gain satisfaction.

He's well on his way to finding purpose.

Thinking about happiness and the pursuit of satisfaction will always bring about emotions.

This is why no one actively does it.

It can make us frustrated or sad when we aren't currently where we'd like to be in life, and no one is yearning to feel this way.

But these emotions caused by thought can also have promise.

Thinking charges us to seek purpose.

What if I told you, right now, how to find purpose in your life? Would you believe me?

Well, today is your lucky day. I can tell you exactly how to find purpose in your life, and it doesn't take a master's degree to understand.

You will absolutely find purpose in your life if you successfully do the following three things:

One
Find what makes you happy

Two
Find what makes you satisfied

Three
Find what you believe in

All of these are founded in thought. Let me explain why each one matters more than anything else you could ever do.

Happiness is short-term.

Finding happiness relies on your ability to surround yourself with people, places, and things (so...nouns) that make you smile and laugh.

Happiness is the momentary feeling of joy as the core emotion.

Satisfaction is long term.

Achieving satisfaction is based on your ability to work on things you find relevant and meaningful.

Belief is overarching.

Finding what you believe in means defining your core values, personal beliefs, and non-negotiables.

If you find yourself seeking purpose. Ask yourself the important questions.

What makes me happy?

What makes me satisfied?

What do I believe in?

Your thoughts will direct your actions, and your actions will direct your outcomes.

When you have thought hard about the questions above, build a life around your answers.

Nothing you ever do could be more meaningful.

Dan has never had a reason to define what he believes. No one has ever asked him what his values are, and even if they would have, he wouldn't have taken the question very seriously.

But now that he's thinking about living a better life, he decides to make a short list of the things he values.

Here are the things he writes down:

- Treat other people right. Don't cheat on my girlfriend, and try to be honest with everyone.
- Take pride in my work. Don't do things half-way.
- Be responsible. If I say I'm going to do something, do it.
- Think about how to be happy and satisfied. Try to put my thoughts into action.

It's a short list, but Dan is happy with it because he now has a few core values to live by. He's no longer floating aimlessly. He is thinking about happiness and removing negative thoughts, working toward accomplishing something meaningful, and defining what he believes.

Dan has started to feel different. He's feeling more in control of his thoughts, and less affected by all the drama. This is when thoughts naturally turn to actions.

There are now skills that Dan needs in order to bring his thoughts to life – to put his positive thoughts into action.

We all want to live a life of purpose. We all want to be happy and feel satisfied with our work. To get there, we need to build our foundational **skills**. The thinking dilemma is not simply about thought; it is about how our thoughts lead to meaningful actions.

While you have hopefully agreed that our thoughts matter, and that you can choose what you think about and how you think about it...

it is our actions that produce results.

We cannot neglect the need to take **action** as a result of our **thoughts**.

We've all spent time in a school setting. We've learned things like math and science. But the **application** of these studies often gets lost.

If you can't apply them to your life, they aren't helpful to you.

Side note: all of these studies can be applied to your life if you **think** enough about how, but that's not where I'm going with this

There are skills that help **every** student excel, no matter their future plans.

I'll tell you what they are, but again, none of these skills matter without our ability to think.

If we don't think well. We don't do well.

We know that thoughts direct our actions; it's time to **act** with purpose.

I'm talking about:

Building the **skills** necessary to align our **thoughts** with our **actions** will help us maximize our happiness, satisfaction, and purpose.

These 8 skills affect everything.

<u>**One**</u>

Communication

Studies show that communication is 55% body language, 38% tone of voice, and only 7% what is actually said.

What you say matters, but **how** you say it matters more.

Sometimes, what you don't say matters most.

When you talk, you are stating what you already know. When you listen, you learn something new.

Knowing how to step back and listen to ideas is essential. An effective communicator takes charge but also gives others a chance to voice their opinions.

How you communicate with the world around you will determine how people respond to your thoughts and actions.

Personal Branding

Your personal brand is made up of the thoughts, feelings, and emotions others have when they interact with you. It is in direct correlation to your sense of identity and how closely your actions align with the way you perceive yourself.

Two questions will tell you everything you need to know:

1. What do you want to be known for?

2. Do your actions align with what you want to be known for?

If you can easily answer question one, and honestly say yes to question two, you've nailed it. If it's not totally clear (which is most of us), read on.

To create and develop your personal brand you must do these four things really well:

Be confident in yourself and your abilities

Let your real personality drive your interactions

Be ready for opportunities to show your identity

Always know your environment

When your actions align with your identity, you are living with purpose. When others perceive your true identity through your actions, you've created a strong personal brand.

Three

Action

Thinking sets the stage for action.

When we only think and never do, we fail.

People will always tell you what they **want** to do. Then they don't do it.

Talking about what you **could** do means absolutely nothing in the long run.

Few things are worse than not living up to your potential.

We've all heard that:

A journey of a thousand miles begins with a single step.

But sometimes we forget that the important part of this is the step.

> Not thinking about the step.
>> Not counting the number of steps in a thousand miles.
>>> Not telling other people that you'd like to walk a long way.

If you want to walk a thousand miles, buy some shoes and **do it.**

And if you just want to make a sports team or be in the play, at the very least you need to try out.

Action separates dreamers from doers.

Don't let your dreams be dreams.

Turn them into reality

Four

Manage Time

When we have found the things that make us happy and satisfied, we must then determine the time we are willing to give to these things.

Balance is always complicated, but at the core of finding balance should always be the pursuit of happiness and satisfaction.

There aren't enough minutes in a day.

Thinking about the most appropriate way to allocate your 1,440 minutes per day matters.

Allocate your time to pursuits that allow you to get the most out of life.

When you do find the pursuits you believe in, put your all into those pursuits and get the results you've dreamed of. Effort matters more than most people want to admit.

Side note: don't stress yourself out. You can't be everywhere or do everything. But you can choose to live with purpose

Five

Work Smarter

Everyone will tell you to work harder, but true efficiency and effectiveness in your daily workings comes from being innovative and approaching life differently.

The best way to **work** smarter is to **get** smarter.

When we push ourselves to learn, our thinking reaches new levels. When our ability to think expands, our actions become more meaningful.

There's an old saying that goes:

You're either getting better or getting worse. You're never staying the same.

Students who learn new things every day and apply their findings to their studies, work, and life set the foundations for happiness, satisfaction, and purpose.

Six

Meet the Right People

There will be at least ten people who will help you between now and the time you accomplish something great.

The right people can change everything. The right teachers, bosses, guidance counselors, colleagues, and friends affect us in ways we often don't realize.

To **meet** the right people, we must **be** the right people.

Ask yourself:
Why would someone want to meet me?

If the answer is:
They wouldn't.

Then you have some work to do.

Once you've done some self-exploration, the key to meeting the **right** people becomes meeting **more** people.

How do you know you've met the right people until you've met some of the wrong ones?

When we diversify our connections, we get new ideas, resources, and avenues to happiness and satisfaction.

Seven

Maintain Relationships

Bridges are always more beautiful when built instead of burnt. We lose when we burn bridges because we'll never be able to cross them again.

The best way to keep our connections is to build **trust-based** relationships with the **right people**.

Trust keeps our relationships, our figurative bridges, strong. It helps us get to the destinations we desire.

Action items to revisit when working to maintain relationships:

Follow up with someone you haven't talked to in awhile.

Don't forget where you came from.

Let others help you build the life of purpose you've envisioned.

Eight

Motivation

Whatever goal you've decided will make you most satisfied, you must not lose your **ambition** in the pursuit of achieving it.

Satisfaction comes from the **completion** of the race, not the **start**.

Determination and perseverance pay off.

If you can't keep yourself motivated, have a trusted friend, teacher, family member, or colleague hold you accountable.

We all need an extra push sometimes.

Happiness, satisfaction, and purpose are difficult to attain.

We cannot lose our drive to achieve great things.

Between goals and results lie discipline and consistency.

If you lack motivation, go back and think about the foundational questions earlier in this book.

Staying motivated is easier when the direction is clear and the reasons are worthy.

Keep in mind that these skills are not helpful without a strong foundation in thought.

When we think about the right things, we give ourselves permission to act accordingly.

And when we've made the decision to act based in positive thought, we give ourselves permission to improve everyday.

Use these eight skills to bring your thoughts to actions, and improve them every day in your pursuit of happiness, satisfaction, and purpose.

Dan has a great start on building these skills. He has already connected with his business teacher and band instructor. They have helped him build his vision for a satisfying life. He has also gotten more motivated to be happy and has communicated this desire to his girlfriend.

Instead of continuing to live in a lull, Dan now has a clearer purpose based in positive thought and stronger values. This purpose, interestingly enough, was there all along, but it took Dan's shift in thinking to realize it.

Then it happens.

Dan goes to a football game to play in the band. All goes well until he sees Tyler and Amy taking their typical post-game-kiss selfie.

"I hate them so much." He can't help it.

His friend next to him chimes in, "They're like a celebrity couple that only cares about their image. It's so stupid."

"I hope they slip in a puddle walking off the field."

The drama is back. The natural, negative default setting has returned, and there was almost nothing Dan could have done to stop it.

The world seems to fight for Dan's thoughts every chance it gets. The world doesn't care that Dan has made decisions about how he wants to think and live.

This is what makes the thinking dilemma so challenging.

Once you have built the foundations for your thoughts and skills, do not let them go.

Fight hard for them because there are opposing forces that will try to keep you from being happy, satisfied, and living a life of purpose.

Distractions

The number one enemy of thought is our own attention.

The most underrated skill in the **world** today is this:

Guarding Our Attention

If we agree that our thoughts matter and that there is a very real thinking dilemma in this world, why do we let anything and everything affect the way we think?

It is incredibly easy for others to direct what we think about and how we think about it.

Which absolutely baffles me.

Have you ever experienced road rage?

We have no idea who the driver of another car is, but as soon as they cut us off, our entire day is ruined. Our mood is altered. Our thoughts turn negative. Our faith in humanity plummets to zero.

But what really happens is this:

Our attention gets stolen.

Attention thieves are everywhere.

Another example: we start the day believing we are going to build the crucial skills necessary to succeed based in positive thought (or we at least think we're going to have a good day), and ten minutes later, we are perusing social media and see something that upsets us. It alters our thoughts which alters the rest of our day.

It happens to everyone, and its time to take a stand.

You are the guardian of your attention. You can give it to whatever or whomever you choose.

When we guard our attention properly, we ignite something that truly makes us better:

Focus

Our ability to focus determines the strength of our thought.

Focused **thinking** begets confident **action**.

When we are focused, we improve. When we are distracted, we get worse.

When we give ourselves an opportunity to focus fully on a thought, we allow ourselves to think deeply, form confident ideas, and bring those ideas to life.

This applies to anything: studying, jobs, learning a new language, improving a jump shot.

We truly improve in a practice when we remove outside distractions and focus.

Thinking is hard. If thinking were easy, we wouldn't have this dilemma.

But thinking is also possible. With effort and focus, our thoughts can prevail.

Dan begins to take efforts to guard his attention. When things initially upset him, he tries hard to stop and ask himself, "Should I really be upset about this? Or is this another distraction from my important thoughts?"

He starts placing his phone on silent when he's practicing the trumpet so he can focus and improve in the way he wants.

He starts to take more ownership of his social media pages so he sees less of the things that slowly ruin his happiness (mostly hiding posts from Tyler and Amy).

Dan has done a great job making himself happier, more satisfied, and has has set the stage for a life of purpose.

He is smiling more and staying out of drama that doesn't align with his intentional thoughts. He understands that he cannot control the world around him, but he can control the way he views it.

The steps he took may not seem revolutionary. They may seem small. But even the smallest of actions based in positive thought strengthen the foundation of a better life.

Dan is in a good place.

But his job is not done.

His girlfriend still has no clue there is a thinking dilemma in this world. Neither do his friends. Dan's life has dramatically improved based solely on his own thoughts. If Dan truly cares about the people around him, he needs to share these thoughts with others so they can work to overcome the thinking dilemma with him.

When Dan shares these thoughts with the people around him, he challenges them to be present and think positively. This creates a snowball effect; the more people who know about the thinking dilemma and work against it in their lives, the happier and more satisfied the world becomes.

Even if they won't admit it, people want what Dan now has. They want to be happy, satisfied, and have lives of purpose, and the good news for Dan is that there is no reason for him to keep the path to this life a secret.

Dan's life has completely changed, and it is one hundred percent because he has become more present, stopped to reflect, and taken control of his thoughts.

I can't tell you what the future holds for Dan, because Dan's future is completely up to him.

But I can tell you that by recognizing the thinking dilemma in this world and actively working to overcome it, he has set the foundation for a life of happiness, satisfaction, and purpose, and there is nothing more important than that.

So we know **why** to think:

Thinking directs our happiness. Thoughts lead to actions, and actions lead to outcomes.

We know **what** to think:

Whatever fits with our vision of the best way to **be** and to **live**.

We know how to find **purpose**:

Find what makes us **happy.**

Find what makes us **satisfied.**

Find what we **believe** in.

We know the foundational **skills** necessary to achieve our goals:

Communication

Personal Branding

Action

Manage Time

Work Smarter

Meet the Right People

Maintain Relationships

Motivation

And we know that being **distracted** from our thoughts gets us nowhere.

The only thing left to do is:

CHOOSE

TO

THINK

We cannot go through life as zombies anymore.

We need to stop relying on others to create our thoughts.

We need to stop communicating like John Madden.

And we need to do it **now**.

We need to put our phones away from time to time.
We need to stop zoning out into video games.
We need to be more positive to others.
We need to think.

The Thinking Dilemma is **Urgent**.

With focused thought backed by core skills, anyone can find happiness, satisfaction, and purpose.

We must think to build lives that matter.

When you take control of your thoughts your world will change.

And now is the time to change your world.

Your thoughts direct your actions; your actions direct your outcomes.

What type of life do you truly want to live?

THINK
ABOUT IT.

Author's Note

Dan could have had a conversation with Tyler or Amy at any time to try to change his perception of them. I chose to keep them completely separated to emphasize that the negative thoughts the two of them elicited in Dan's mind were not relevant to Dan in any way. They were Dan's "attention thieves."

Attention thieves may hit closer to home in our lives than they did in Dan's life. While Dan had an issue with people who did not play an active role in his day-to-day life, you may have issues with teammates, bosses, parents, teachers, etc. These people, because they play a more active role in your life, make the thinking dilemma much more difficult to overcome.

The points in this book still apply. Whether your distractions are far off (Tyler and Amy) or nearby (a teacher), you have the ability to build the life you envision based in positive thoughts.

I've often heard that life is 10% what happens to you and 90% how you respond to it. This is a nice cliché, but it is much easier said than done. Responding to issues with positivity and building a life of happiness, satisfaction, and purpose is hard. It is incredibly hard. It is so hard that most people could spend a lifetime thinking about these things and not reach concrete answers.

I would still argue that the time taken thinking about these items is not wasted time. Stopping to reflect, analyze, and change our surroundings is a helpful practice for anyone and everyone.

Choosing to think matters for all of us.

About the Author

Kyle Willkom is the founder of Action Packed Leadership. He is a thought leader in the area of life skill development and speaks around the country for audiences of all sizes.

A graduate of Marquette University, Kyle spent two-and-a-half years full-time with FOCUS Training speaking and running workshops on topics such as teambuilding, goal setting, and effective communication. He then spent close to a year helping build the marketing startup, Sabljak Raether Hogerton, before founding Action Packed Leadership.

Kyle's first book, Wake Up Call, was a best seller for FOCUS Training, and has reached students across the country as well as internationally.

To hire Kyle as a keynote speaker, workshop presenter, or to see more of Kyle's content:

Visit
ActionPackedLeadership.com.

Also by Kyle Willkom

Wake Up Call
5 Essential Lessons They Won't Teach You in School

A novel about Dillon, a student whose life gets turned upside down by an unexpected twist of fate. His next steps lead him on a fantastical journey that teaches him life-changing lessons he could not have learned any other way.

Learn more at:
ActionPackedLeadership.com

Works Cited

Covey, Stephen. *The 7 Habits of Highly Effective People.* New York: Free Press. 1989. Print.

Docter, Pete. (Director). *Inside out.* Motion picture.

Ferrazzi, Keith. *Never Eat Alone.* New York City: Boubleday, 2005. Print.

Horn, Sam. "What is the Eyebrow Test?" *The Intrigue Agency.* The Intrigue Agency, 3 Feb. 2012. Web. 7 June 2014. <http://samhornpop.wordpress.com/>.

Horsager, David. "You Can't Be a Great Leader Without Trust. Here's How You Build It." *Forbes.* Forbes Magazine, 24 Oct. 2012. Web. 22 July 2014. <http://www.forbes.com/sites/forbesleadershipforum/2012/10/24/you-cant-be-a-great-leader-without-trust-heres-how-you-build-it/>.

Kreitzer, Mary Joe. "Why Personal Relationships are Important." *University of Minnesota.* Regents of the University of Minnesota and Charlson Meadows, n.d. Web. 11 August, 2014. <http://www.takingcharge.csh.umn.edu/enhance-your-wellbeing/relationships/why-personal-relationships-are-important>.

Lenhart, Amanda, Rich Ling, Scott Campbell, and Kristen Purcell. "Teens and Mobile Phones." *Pew Research Center: Internet, Science, and Tech.* Pew Research Center, 20 April 2012. Web. 16 June 2014. <http://www.pewinternet.org/2010/04/20/teens-and-mobile-phones/>.

Llopis, Glenn. "Personal Branding Is A Leadership Requirement, Not a Self-Promotion Campaign." *Forbes.* Forbes Magazine, 8 April 2013. Web. 2 July 2014. <http://www.forbes.com/sites/glennllopis/2013/04/08/personal-branding-is-a-leadership-requirement-not-a-self-promotion-campaign/>.

Marr, Bernard. "If You Want to Impress a Stranger, Here Are the Body Language Mistakes to Avoid." *Quartz.* Quartz, 9 July 2014. Web. 14 July 2014. <http://qz.com/231866/here-are-the-body-language-mistakes-you-should-avoid-making-with-strangers/>.

Matthews, Joe, Don Debolt and Deb Percival. "10 Time Management Tips that Work." *Entrepreneur.* Entrepreneur Media, Inc., n.d. Web. 16 July 2014. <http://www.entrepreneur.com/article/219553>.

Mehrabian, Albert. *Nonverbal Communication.* Chicago: Aldine-Atherton, 1972. Print.

"Networking." *Yale Office of Career Strategy.* Yale University, 2014. Web. 11 July 2014. <http://ucs.yalecollege.yale.edu/content/networking>.

"Study Focuses on Strategies for Achieving Goals, Resolutions." *Dominican University of California.* Dominican University of Califiornia, n.d. Web. 3 July 2014. <http://www.dominican.edu/dominicannews/study-backs-up-strategies-for-achieving-goals>.

Vaynerchuk, Gary. "You're Focusing on the Wrong Stuff." *Medium.* Gary Vaynerchuk, 28 May 2014 Web. 7 July 2014. <https://medium.com/@garyvee/youre-focusing-on-the-wrong-stuff-543aed6168e5>.

Vaynerchuk, Gary. "Why Frowning is Better than Smiling." *Medium.* Gary Vaynerchuk, 7 April 2014 Web. 7 July 2014. <https://medium.com/the-entrepreneurs-journey/why-frowning-is-better-than-smiling-c1c1f76362f3#.an73emifh>.

Made in the USA
Lexington, KY
05 May 2016